Closing Times

Sheffield Public Houses

as they were . . .

. . . and what's there now

Volume 1

Printed by Pickards.org.uk

Unit 5, Edmund Road Business Centre, 135 Edmund Road, Sheffield S2 4ED

Telephone 0114 275 7222

email: mliversidge@pickards.org.uk

www.pickards.org.uk

About twenty years ago my father, Michael Liversidge, produced a book entitled The A-Z of Sheffield Public Houses. The book was well received by the people of Sheffield and sold reasonably well for a small print run, local interest, book.

Albeit disinterested at the time, I have come to notice that the book which included over 600 images and small profiles or simple addresses has seen closures of around 400 of the hostelries that were still serving when my father was a frequent pub goer.

Using over 100 of his original colour images (the A-Z book was printed in mono (black and White) only, so some of these images will be seen in colour for the first time) I have tried to find the exact locations of some of these now demolished drinking establishments to produce a THEN AND NOW format book. Places like the Broughton Inn which was sited where the corner of the Sheffield Motorpoint Arena car park now stands - The Hole in the Wall now literally, itself, a hole in the wall just before the Wicker, The Hare and Hounds Nursery Street where, at the time just before going to press, I took an image of the rubble of the demolished pub with just the letter H of the pub sign still on view. The Beehive in Wadsley is now a Tesco supermarket which the last landlady stated was the very reason for the closure, cheap alcohol. Other now defunct old pubs are being used as businesses, turned into apartments, flats and houses. A prime example is the Haychatter Inn in Bradfield which is now a private dwelling known as the Haychatter House. The Furnival on Verdon Street has been re-launched as a religious establishment The Methodist Church of Sheffield.

Golden Ball, Attercliffe Road from and original image by Gary Mackender

My father has kept a curious, helpful, eye on the development of the book which without his original images would, obviously, not have been possible.

I hope you are reminded of some of the good times you had in these old Sheffield public houses and hopefully go out and take some photographs yourself of the places that are there one minute and gone the next. Go on get your cameras out.

The list within the book is in alphabetical order A to L of Sheffield public houses. List M to Y will be in volume two.

Mark R. Liversidge

NOW
2017

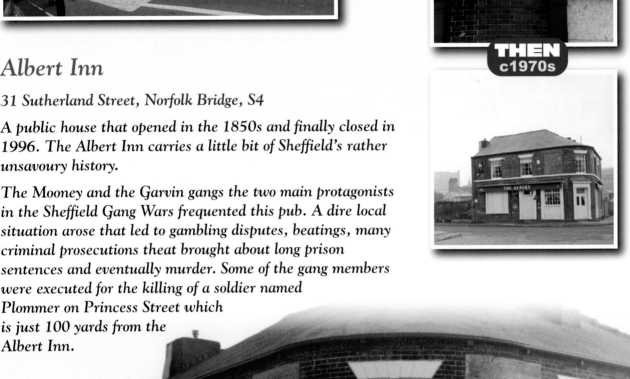

THEN
c1970s

Albert Inn

31 Sutherland Street, Norfolk Bridge, S4

A public house that opened in the 1850s and finally closed in 1996. The Albert Inn carries a little bit of Sheffield's rather unsavoury history.

The Mooney and the Garvin gangs the two main protagonists in the Sheffield Gang Wars frequented this pub. A dire local situation arose that led to gambling disputes, beatings, many criminal prosecutions theat brought about long prison sentences and eventually murder. Some of the gang members were executed for the killing of a soldier named Plommer on Princess Street which is just 100 yards from the Albert Inn.

THEN
1984

NOW 2017

The Albion

4 Mitchell Street - Brooke Drive, S3

A well frequented Tetley public house that is now no longer serving the local drinkers as well as the many University students who found the Albion a comfortable venue.

To keep its connection with the Sheffield University the old building has now been transformed into student accommodation (left).

THE ALBION

FISH AND CHIPS

THEN c1980s

THEN c1980s

The Albion

2-4 Earsham Street, Spital Hill, S4

Originally called the Albion Hotel, pictured above, it was also known as the Golden Perch, Old Mill Tavern and Mill Tavern.

The Albion was one of the few six day houses in Sheffield meaning it always closed on Sundays.

Now being used as shops and a travel agency.

NOW 2017

THEN c1990s

THEN c1990s

THEN c1980s

Alexandra Hotel

549 Carlisle Street East, S9

Public house that closed in the mid 1970s left derelict for quite some time, (above), before being demolished.

The Alexandra can be seen in the image (top right) when a large fire engulfed the nearby steel firm.

It was originally built sometime in the 1860s.

Postcard shown right was a personal card printed by the then Landlord Joshua Smith.
At that time it was selling
Strout's Noted Ales.

THEN c1930s

JOSHUA SMITH.
ALEXANDRA HOTEL, CARLISLE STREET EAST,
SHEFFIELD.

THEN c1970s

NOW 2017

NOW 2017

The Alexandra

Exchange Street, Castlegate, S2

A Bass Tavern public house and hotel that closed a few years ago and is now advertising itself as luxury student accommodation. The Alexandra Hotel, at the junction of Exchange Street and Castle Gate, had stood empty, but after a redesign by an architectural firm it is now a 23 studio complex complete with gym.

Originally named after Edward VII wife, Alexandra who also gave her name to six more so named public houses within Sheffield.

THEN c2000s

The Arbourthorne

6 Errington Road, S2

Unsure if the information we are passing on is correct but we heard it on the grapevine that Marc Bolan once appeared at the Arbourthorne c1975.

The visit was as a promotional tour - and although he was on his way down by this point, I would imagine Marc Bolan at The Arbourthorne Hotel was pretty big news at the time. Reliably informed that at one point he was stood on the rooftop and throwing promotional T shirts to the onlookers.

Image top right shows all that is left of the Arbourthorne pub sign on the new redevelopment site.

The Atlas

Bawtry Road, Brinsworth

A John Smiths public house that was originally built as the living accommodation for the Rotherham Main Colliery manager. It also had stables for the ponies and horses that were used down and around the pit. The stables were used, at one time, as the local mortuary.

The Atlas was a beer serving establishment, in the Brinsworth area, for well over a century.

The old public house building was demolished and a new property, Atlas Court, has taken its place on the local landscape.

The Ball

287 Darnall Road, S9

Built around 1910 this John Smiths public house has been left for some considerable time to become a decaying eyesore for the locals of Darnall. It is a Grade II listed building but is in desperate need of repair.

It is one of the tallest structures in Darnall and at one time was reputed to have its own ghost. Local legend has it that it was a young women who hung herself from the attic rafters when she found out she had fallen pregnant.

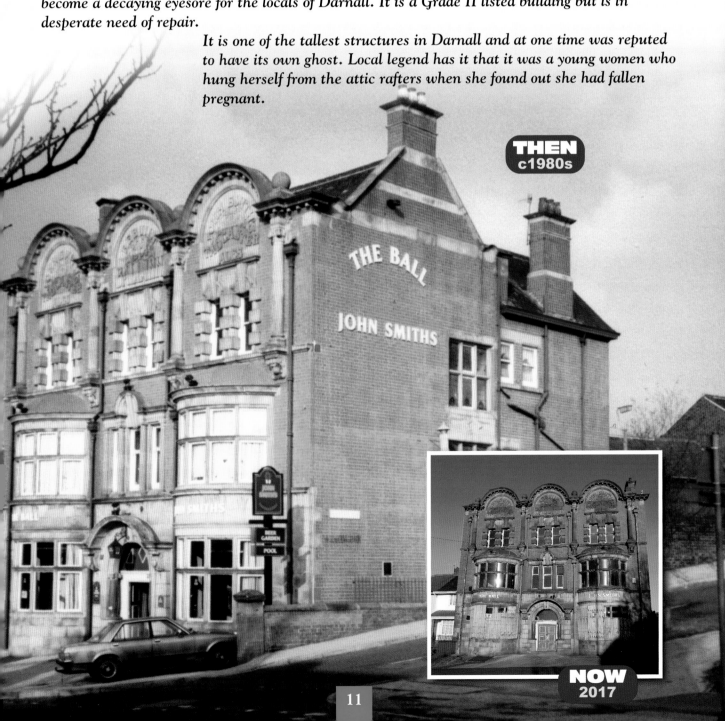

The Ball Inn now the Milestone

84 Green Lane and on the corner of Ball Street, S3

The Ball Inn was in a derelict state for many years and used by different businesses until it rose like a phoenix from the flames as the Milestone a wonderful restaurant/public house.

The original Ball Inn public house was opened in the 1830s.

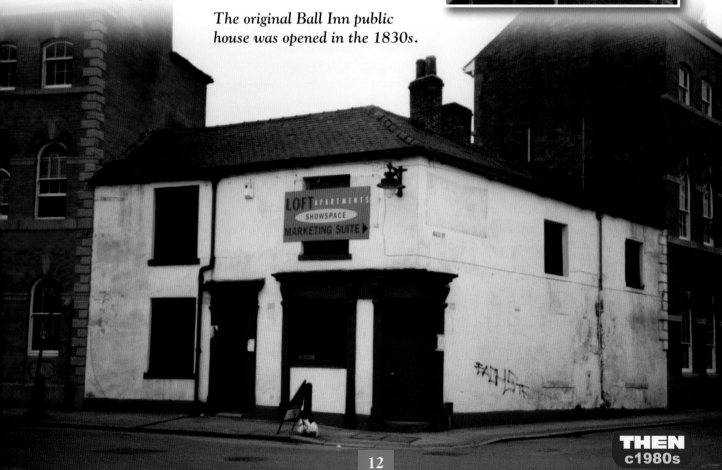

THEN
c1980s

Ball Inn

230 Myrtle Road, Heeley, S2

A Tetleys public house that in 2015 saw new plans submitted to turn this former pub, The Ball Inn, into flats, and build a new block of apartments.

Proposals were lodged that the Myrtle Road public house be turned into five flats, and put up 11 apartments on the site. However, the application was later withdrawn. Now the previous scheme has been redesigned to reduce the size, as well as to simplify the design of the new block. At the time of going to press this development has not started.

NOW
2017

The Ball

106 High Street, Ecclesfield

The Ball was a well frequented public house for many years when along with the Greyhound, Black Bull, White Bear, Griffin, Stocks/Tankard the village of Ecclesfield was very well served with beer serving establishments. Now only three of these six mentioned pubs still operate.

Although now closed to the drinking public of Ecclesfield this pub was one of an inordinate amount of public houses called The Ball within Sheffield boundaries. No other city or town in England had as many public houses named The Ball. Along with the many variances like Golden Ball, Blue Ball, Ball in Tree etc.

Still in a derelict condition (above) as we go to press.

THEN
c1980s

Barcentro

Cambridge Street, S1

This shortlived bar was opened in the late 1990s and survived less than 20 years. It was sited next to Henrys Bar and probably suffered from the plethora of pubs old and new situated around it.

As mentioned; Henrys Bar next door, Sportsman, Wapentake (Casbah), Yorkshireman, Benjamin Huntsman and Lloyds No 1 were all within less than a hundreds yards or so.
Now a sad looking building that will, hopefully, soon see a renovation.

THEN
c2000s

NOW
2017

Bathfield

Powell Street and Weston Street, S3

A Wards Brewery public house that was opened in 1965 and closed around 2003. It catered for the locals of the nearby Netherthorpe Flats and also the student population of Sheffield University.

The three storey building, picture, has taken the place of the former Bathfield public house and now, I believe, contains 9 student apartments and communal gardens.

THEN
c1980s

The Beehive

Dykes Hall Road, S6

The smoking ban and competition from cheap supermarket chains were the final nails in the Beehives coffin, according to a former landlady. The Beehive pub in Dykes Hall Road, Wisewood, was the third public house in the area to close in between 2006-2008 - following The Dial House and The Horse and Jockey. The landlady said she had been forced to call time because of a dramatic drop in customer numbers and also blamed cheap beer in nearby Hillsborough and the impact of the no smoking ban. Ironically the Beehive became, as shown above, a Tesco supermarket.

NOW 2017

Beeley Wood

500-502 Middlewood Road, S6

A Tetleys public house that closed and the building has now been taken over by the Steel City Muscle Gym.

A well frequented public house whose client base was mainly from the Winn Garden area of Middlewood.

THE BEELEY WOOD

PUBMASTER

THEN c2000s

THEN 1980s

THE BEELEY WOOD

TETLEY ALES

Belle Vue

282 Whitehouse Lane, Walkley, S6

A John Smiths, Magnet Ales public house that stood vacant for quite a while and has now been turned into private accommodation. The location of this Public House, was at the top of Walkey Road, and when open guaranteed great views over Hillfoot, Parkwood Springs and across to the Sheffield City Centre.

NOW 2017

Belle Vue Hotel

229 Cricket Inn Road, S2

A Whitbreads public house that is being, at the time of going to press, renovated - as yet I cannot find out for what or into what it is being developed.

The pub itself was a two storey detached public house. The bar area was open plan around a central servery and there was three bedroom living accommodation above.

THEN
c1980s

Bell Hagg

Manchester Road

A Whitbreads public house that is now a private dwelling.

Built in 1832 for Doctor Hodgson.

This was built to antagonise the Vicar of Stannington who had turned down a large donation to his church because the doctor had gained it through gambling.

Hodgson built this 5 story structure as a visual reminder to the vicar who could see it from his church. For many years it was know as Hodgson's folly.

From Manchester Road it seems like a nice 2 storey structure but seen from Stannington you can see that is has 3 more levels, shown left.

Closed as a public house over 10 years ago and now after years of dereliction turned into private dwelling.

21

NOW 2017

Black Swan

39-41 Snig Hill, S1

The original Black Swan started serving the people of Sheffield way back in 1774. Fifty years later it was purchased by the John Crich of Black Rock.

Almost 200 years later the likes of Joe Cocker, Wolves, Rainbow, Jigsaw, The Fortunes and many more popular music acts played at this well known music venue. Three of the acts mentioned went on to have number one UK hit singles.

Also know as: Mucky Duck, Compleat Angler and Boardwalk

THEN c1980s

NOW
2017

NOW
2017

THEN
c1990s

Boomerang

Fawcett Street, Netherthorpe, S3

A public house that was built in the middle part of last century and only just lasted to see its 40th birthday.

The property was converted, in 2002, into student accommodation,

THEN
1984

Bradway

Bradway Road, Sheffield, S17

The original public house was built to quench the thirst of the Irish Navvies who were employed to cut the railway tunnel from Totley to Dronfield. The navvies were originally called miners and the first name of this public house was the Miner's Inn. The building shown (below) was erected in 1920 and only called the Bradway a good few years later. Now a new build (above) is a Sainsbury's Local supermarket.

Bridge Inn

509 London Road, S2

A Wards public house that was built around the 1930s replacing an older same named pub that had stood on this site for well over a century.

In the last decade or so the Bridge Inn has closed and has now been taken over by Greyspace Flooring.

THEN
c1980s

Bridge Inn

2 Meadow Hall Road, S9

This Wards public house was closed and then demolished some years ago. It used to have images of bridges of the world adorning its interior walls.

It has a small claim to fame, in that Dr David Bellamy, for his TV programme visited to investigate the fact that on the bank of the River Don, which runs alongside the pub, it has a fig tree which had grown and overlooked the pubs backyard. A very unusual event in the cooler climate of this country.

NOW 2017

Britannia Inn

22-26 Worksop Road, Attercliffe, S9

On the historical side, this pub housed one of Sheffield's most famous sons, Benjamin Huntsman the man who fathered the steelmaking industry in Sheffield. It is reputed that Huntsman himself made the 24 inch high, 1772, steel numbers that adorned the side of this pub. The old pub stands derelict at the moment.

History Trails Plaque with relevant details (right).

LOWER DON VALLEY
BRITANNIA INN
BELIEVED TO HAVE BEEN
THE HOME OF BENJAMIN
HUNTSMAN (1704-1776) INVENTOR
OF CRUCIBLE STEEL, AND FOUNDER
OF SHEFFIELD'S REPUTATION FOR
QUALITY STEEL. THE DATE
1772 RECORDS THE SETTING
UP OF HIS NEARBY
ATTERCLIFFE WORKS
HISTORY TRAILS S.C.C.

1772

THEN c1980s

NOW 2017

THEN c1900s

Broughton Inn

242 Attercliffe Common or 1 Broughton Lane, S9

A Tetleys public house that closed in the 1970s. This pub, below, stood where the Arena Car Park is now situated. Also where the Sheffield area finishing line was in the Tour de France race. The older Broughton Inn, above left, stood on the opposite corner of Broughton Lane.

The public house takes its name from a Lincolnshire farmer turned highwayman named Spence Broughton. Broughton along with John Oxley robbed the Royal Mail coach in 1791 supposedly on Attercliffe Common. Broughton was caught and hanged at York on 3rd April 1792. The very next day his body was brought back to the spot where the crime had taken place and displayed in a gibbet which kept his rotting remains on show for over 25 years before rotting away. A rather stark deterrent.

The Noose and Gibbet public house (previously The Railway) on Broughton Lane has a gibbet on show. (above right).

THEN c1980s

Brunswick Hotel

30 Tilford Road, Woodhouse

A Whitbreads public house that closed quite a few years ago now and has been opened as a One Stop Shop which serves the local Woodhouse community.

I believe it was a NISA store previously.

The Brunswick was a well frequented local until it went the way of most Sheffield pubs and couldn't cope with cheap alcohol on sale out various outlets. Sky TV and other similar channels also heralded the death knell of many public houses.

The Brunswick used to have a good few historical pictures of Woodhouse around its interior walls.

The Bull and Oak - Brown Cow

76-78 The Wicker and 68 The Wicker, S3

The Bull and Oak pub disappeared to make way for the Derek Dooley Way that runs from the Parkway through into Shalesmoor.

The Bull and Oak itself was closed and demolished in 1998

The Brown Cow building still survives but now as a fast food outlet.

NOW
2017

THEN
c1980s

30

NOW 2017

Bulldog

387 Attercliffe Road, S9

The Tetleys public house shown below was built sometime after the Second World War in the late 1950s or early 1960s and survives now as The Pandoras. Originally the site was occupied by the Bridge (right). The Bridge received a direct hit that not only destroyed the pub but severely damaged the Washroad Bridge on which it stood.

THEN c1920s

Original photograph courtesy Andrea Torbet

THEN c1980s

Burgoyne Arms

246 Langsett Road, S6

A Stones public house that closed c2012 and has been left in the interim to become derelict, above.

Probably named after Lady Burgoyne whose family were Lords of the Manor of Owlerton.

NOW
2017

Cambridge

452 Penistone Road, S6

A John Smiths public house that closed to make way for a road widening project

Situated at the rear of Hillsborough Barracks, on Penistone Road, and named after Adolphus Frederick, Duke of Cambridge, 7th son of King George III.

Flooded and badly damaged by the Great Sheffield Flood of 1864, demolished mid 1990's.

A Renault showrooms stand on this site now.

THEN
c1980s

Cannon

Castle Street

A William Stones public house that now remains derelict.

A lovely old building that was sometimes let down by it customer base and I believe closed, in 2007, because of disruptive behaviour and substance misuse.

The Cannon sign is being slowly covered in foliage which is now, slowly, overtaking the building.

NOW 2017

THEN 1984

Cannon Hall

Barnsley Road, Fir Vale, S5

A Whitbreads public house that closed quite a few years ago and left for a time before being demolished and developed into the tyres business it houses today (right).

The pub also has a ghost, named Charlotte, who according to local legend died of a broken heart and continued to roam the Cannon Hall.

At one time a Karate Club used to be held in the Concert Room.

NOW 2017

THEN c1980s

Captive Queen

131 Guildford Avenue, S2

A Stones public house that closed a good few years ago and was purchased and refurbished as the Sheffield Christian Centre.

The pub stood opposite the Manor House were Mary Queen of Scots was once held prisoner.

THEN 1985

NOW 2017

Catherine Arms

29-31Catherine Street, S3

A Tetley public house that was closed by the police in the 1990s for trouble with absenteeism of the licensee and being linked with drug dealing.

The Sheffield Star reported "One of Sheffields Notorious Blackspot pubs" Attercliffe police stated that "It was known to attract drug dealers, and it would be nice to think there may be a turndown in drug dealing in the area in the light of the decision to close the Catherine".

Now the area is used for private dwellings, shown above.

THEN c1980s

NOW
2017

Charles Turnbull

Liberty Hill, Stannington, S6

A Tetleys public house that was originally called The Charles Turnbull and built in the 1960s.

The pub name was later shortened to just The Turnbull for some mysterious reason.

Mr Turnbull himself was the main director of the Tetleys Brewery company.

It was closed about 10-15 years ago and is now being used as a child care centre.

THEN
c1980s

NOW
2017

THEN
c2000s

Cocked Hat

73-75 Worksop Road, S9

A Marston's public house that closed and at the time of going to press it has been left as pictured (top) awaiting either demolition or renovation.

At least it had a longer lifespan than the Sheffield Stadium (pictured top right) that was built for the Sheffield Student Games in 1991 which only lasted about 20 years.

Cocked Hat interior image (right).

THEN
c1980s

THEN c2000s

NOW 2017

Commercial

3 Sheffield Road, S9

A Wards public house that closed and left for a very long time before being demolished.

Originally built on land know as Woodcrofts in 1870 the Inn was a dwelling house and brewery sited in the township of Tinsley. It use to be a few doors away from the old tram shed and many of the 40s and 50s customers were tram drivers and conductors

THEN c1980s

NOW
2017

Corner Pin

235 Carlisle Street East, S4

A Wards public house that closed to the drinking public in the early 2000s and has now been redeveloped into business premises.

The Corner Pin has stood the test of time being first licensed to sell alcohol in 1840.

The Corner Pin was one of 26 public houses that adorned the three quarter mile stretch of Carlisle Street East that also housed numerous steel and heavy industry firms.

THEN
c1980s

Cossack

45 Howard Street, S1

The Cossack situated on Howard Street just a few doors up from the Howard Street Hotel pictured (centre).

The nearby wall has been decorated with, I believe, an image of Harry Brearley the inventor of Stainless Steel.

The Cossack name came from a Derby winner in 1847 rather than the skilled warriors of the Russian Steppes.

THEN c1980s

Cricket Inn

317 Cricket Inn Road, S2

The Cricket Inn was built in 1936 to serve the new estate. The name of the pub probably comes from a cricket ground that was first used in 1826 when a team of Yorkshire cricketers played a Norfolk X1. The ground was later transformed into the Hyde Park Greyhound Stadium.

This Bass Charrington public house that closed many years ago and left for a time as above before being demolished. The area has now been developed as a shopping retail park.

Cross Guns

122 Sharrow Lane - 115 Franklin Street

A Tetleys public house that closed many years ago and now being used as a builders and engineering business premises, I believe, for Dendale Ltd.

Previously known as the Great Gun.

NOW 2017

Crown

2 Walkley Bank Road, S6

A Tetleys public house that closed c2014 and has now been turned into nice individual dwellings within the aptly named Crown House.

The information that was once given on the pubs website:
The Crown Inn is a quiet pub that is ideal for a relaxing drink with friends. Inside you will find a friendly atmosphere and if you fancy a few frames they also have their own snooker table.

THEN c1980s

NOW
c2000s

Crown

116 Neepsend Lane, S3

A William Stones public house that at one time was used as the tap for the William Stones brewery which can be seen in the background (top).

The Rutland Hotel was originally sited on the corner of Rutland Road and Neepsend Lane (centre) and the original Crown Inn was sited facing the Gardner Rest (below)

THEN
c1940s

THEN
c1950s

Crown

116 Neepsend Lane, S3

A public house that was a very well frequented dinnertime and evening venue for the many steelworkers who were employed in the numerous steel and other industries that littered the Neepsend area of Sheffield. From the larger employees of Samuel Osbornes, Neepsend Steel and Tool, The Stones Brewery itself to the smaller businesses Jenkinson Marshall & Co.Ltd printers, La Pla who occupied the old Monkey Works, previously the Victoria public house, Wells Richardson Chartered Accountants who eventually took over the old Cannon House pictured on the right of the bottom image

THEN
c1980s

THE CROWN   STONES

The Crown

THE CROWN INN

Crown Inn

Forncett Street, Harleston Street

A Wards public house that closed a good few year ago and was for sale for a while before becoming a business premises (top)

Cuthbert Bank

Langsett Road

A William Stones public house that closed c2013 and left to fall into dereliction. It is shuttered up at the moment, so hopefully it may rise from the ashes but that is doubtful. New building is being erected adjacent to the old pub so keep watching for development

NOW
2017

Cutlers Arms

Worksop Road

A Stones public house that closed and reopened a couple of times. Originally the Cutlers Arms and later renamed Faras (right) and left for period before, I believe, becoming a private dwelling.

My grandfather Joe Liversidge photographed outside Faras in central image.

THEN
c1990s

FARA'S

Cutlers Arms

Stones

THEN
c1980s

NOW
2017

Deerstalker

252 Deer Park Road, Stannington, S6

A public house that lasted about 50-60 years from new build to closure.

The Deerstalker, after closure, was then renovated to accommodate a business called Personal Trainers Inc. They have a fully equipped, air conditioned private gym which opens 7 days per week.

THEN
c1980s

THEN
c2000s

Deep End
now Rawson Spring

Langsett Road, S6

The old Hillsborough and Walkley Baths was converted into a public house aptly named the Deep End by the Tom Cobleigh company in the 1990s. It was renovated using some of the old tiled cubicles. It never really worked and thankfully the saviour of old, large, buildings Wetherspoons stepped in and not only saved the place but renovated it to a much higher standard with better beer prices and as with all "spoons" pubs; good grub. A very busy public house every day of the week but even more so on match days when Sheffield Wednesday, who play nearby, are at home.

Images (above) taken when workmen were putting the long bar in place and transforming the public house from the Deep End to Wetherspoons Rawson Spring.

THEN
c2000s

NOW c2017

THEN c2012

Above: Large Open plan main room in Rawson Spring.

Above Left: Pub Sign

Left: Rawson Spring FC successful local football team winning league and cup competitions around 2012-14 in the Sheffield Meadowhall League

The Rawson Spring

NOW c2017

THEN c1990s

NOW 2017

SEASONS GREETINGS
WENDY & ALAN
"THE DENISON"
SHEFFIELD

Denison Arms

33 Watery Street, 64 Malinda Street, S3

A public house that closed many years ago and has now been replaced with the flats/apartments (pictured above right). Previously known as The Old House at Home.

Small wallets that landlord /landlady gave free to the locals (right).

THEN c1980s

DENISON   The Denison   ARMS

Devonshire Arms

118 Ecclesall Road, S11

A Wards public house that was on Ecclesall Road opposite the brewery that supplied the Devonshire with its beer.

The Devonshire Arms went the way of other nearby pubs; New Inn, Earl Grey, Jolly Buffer and the Little Mesters. Five more Sheffield public houses that are now no more.

The Devonshire Arms was one of four public houses with the same name within the Sheffield boundaries.

The building was erected in 1840

Ecclesall Gate building is now sited where "the Dev" was.

THEN c1980s

THEN c1990s

NOW 2017

NOW 2017

Dog and Partridge

Attercliffe Road

A William Stones public house that has been closed for many years. It saw a very brief resurgence when being turned into a gentlemens club, Sapphire Lounge, but now, at the time of going to print, seems to be awaiting a new investor/buyer.

A pub that was well known, in the 1950-1970s by the locals of Attercliffe as an establishment that could get a little bit boisterous.

THEN c1980s

DOMINO HOUSE

Domino

Egerton Street, S1

A Wards public house that opened in 1970 and did not see it through to the Millennium. A 25-28 year span is short by any standards but I do think this is one of the shortest lifetime for a pub we have witnessed in Sheffield. In 1997 a new building was due to replace the old Domino and accommodate flats for students.

Domino House is part of a 65 bedroom complex with Egerton and Headford houses.

Aerial view of the old pub (right).

THE DOMINO

THEN c1980s

WARDS

The Domino

WARDS

NOW 2017

THEN c1990s

Durham Ox

15 Cricket Inn Road, S2

A Tetley house that has been in decline/disrepair for almost 25-30 year with, at present, no signs of any renovation or demolition taking place. The pub opened in 1862 and closed in 1993.

The name of the pub, The Durham Ox is named after a superior type of Ox bred by Charles Collings a well known cattle breeder from Darlington.

THEN c1980s

Earl of Arundel and Surrey

528 Queens Road, S2

A Tetleys public house that closed and was developed into the Giant Store, a large cycle selling outlet.

The Earl of Arundel and Surrey was a Pound Pub which meant that the landlord was required, by an Act of Parliament to take stray animals into his care - the legal instruction was: "Keep a stable and provender for any stray animals which the police or any other authority cared to bring at any time of day or night".

THEN c1980s

NOW 2017

Earl Francis

64 Manor Oaks Road, S2

A small concrete public house that has now been re-developed into the Earl Francis convenience store, opened in 2012.

This Tetley's pub closed its doors as a pubic house in the 1990s

THEN c1980s

NOW 2017

Earl George

61 The Pavement, S2

Another public house that was built into the large flat complexes that were sited around the Sheffield area.

This Tetleys house has now disappeared into the new refurbished Park Hill flats/homes/businesses complex and is now the Grace Owen children's nursery.

THEN c1980s

East House

18 Spital Hill, S4

Having had a license for over 100 years it is unfortunate that the East House will probably go down in the history books of Sheffield for a Somalian named Mohamed Ishmail who walked into the pub on New Years Day 1960 with a loaded revolver and emptied all 6 bullets into customers who were getting ready to celebrate the New Year. Three died at the scene and two more were seriously injured. The police found the killer hiding in the toilets with an excuse that he wanted to commit suicide but his religious beliefs forbade this so he thought the British would hang him. No such luck as he was deported back to Somolia after only 6 months. Good old British justice.

THEN
c1980s

Enfield Arms

95 Broughton Lane, S9

A Tetleys public house that closed around 2007.

This public house was at one time owned by the Sheffield Ice Hockey team the Sheffield Steelers. Where supporters meeting and events used to take place.

One of the four public houses on a 150 yard stretch of Broughton Lane along with the Broughton Inn, Bird in Hand, The Railway and the Enfield itself.

The demolished site that was were the Enfield stood, centre image.

NOW
2017

THEN
c1990s

NOW 2017

Engineers

2 Fife Street, Wincobank

aka Barrow House, Dallas Bar

A public house that served the people of lower Wincobank for many years including the workers at Arthur Lees. The pub had a few name changes in it history - over the years it has been known as The Barrow House, pictured below and the Dallas Bar. One can understand the Barrow House name as the pub is on the corner of Barrow Street but the Dallas Bar seems very strange.

One of the old windows had
a lovely engraved advertisement for
Berrys Lion Ales

The site is now a used car sale business.

THEN c1980s

NOW
2017

Excelsior

1 Carbrook Street and Attercliffe Common, S9

The original pub was refurbished, by Wards Brewery, in the 1970 an undertaking that doubled the size of the establishment.

A Wards public house that closed some years ago for road widening, and demolished in 1993. It was probably demolished for no reason as lo and behold the widening that took place did not encroach onto the land where the Excelsior stood and the plot is still unoccupied.

THEN
c1980s

NOW
2017

Farfield (aka Owl, Muff Inn)

376 Neepsend Lane, Hillfoot Bridge

A Tetleys public house that closed and has stood slowly fading into disrepair over a 10 year period.

During April 1864 a wall of water about ten feet high swept past the Farfield possible higher than the wording just about the windows on the bottom image. This was during the Great Sheffield Flood that killed over 240 of the local inhabitants.

Outdoor toilets (right).

NOW
c2013

THEN
c1980s

Fellbrigg

331 Arbourthorne Road, S2

A Tetleys public house that long since closed and has been developed as The Beacon church and community centre.

In the 1960s the Fellbrigg and Horse and Lion were the places to be seen. Two very fashionable pubs in their day.

THEN
c1990s

Fiery Fred

Clipstone Gardens off Coleridge Road, S9

The Fiery Fred was opened by Fred Trueman himself in 1982.

He took over 300 wickets for England in a long and illustrious cricketing career.

The image at the bottom of the page has its sign showing the fast bowler in action.

The name was changed a good few years later to the Greenland, possibly because of it location to Greenland Road.

The old pub now stands in disrepair.

NOW
2017

THEN
c1980s

Firth Park Hotel

127 Page Hall Road, S5

A large well frequented pub that used to be one of many such premises in this area all of which, I believe, are now gone. No other public houses now remain in the Firth Park, Fir Vale, Shiregreen or Upwell Street areas.

The Firth Park Hotel has now been purchased by the Pakistan Community Association (above).

NOW 2017

Five Arches Hotel

Herries Road, S5

A Whitbreads public house that was built around 1936 and was a mainstay of the local Southey, Longley and Herries community until the latter years of its lifetime in the 2000s. The pub was named after the Wardsend Viaduct which is sited further down Herries Road.

A frequently visited pub in the 1980s for the author of this book, especially on Friday nights.

It was reported, in the Sheffield Star, that the pub had a ghostly visitation or in this case five ghostly shapes caught on camera when the then landlady, Diane Knell captured the images on cctv.

The site is now being used by the Herries Lodge Care Home, (above).

THEN c1980s

Foundry Arms

111 Barrow Road, S9

A Tetleys public house that managed to fight its corner longer than most of its contemporaries but eventually decided to hang up it gloves.

In its heyday it was a well frequented and welcoming place to have a pint.

Now a tanning, toning, beauty treatment business name Revitalise.

THEN
c1980s

NOW 2017

Fox and Duck

174 Pye Bank Road

A Tetleys public house that closed a good few years ago and was left for a time as pictured below before finally being demolished.

This piece of land is now derelict, (above).

THEN c1980s

THEN c1980s

THEN c1990s

NOW
2017

Fox and Duck

Sheffield Road, Tinsley, S9

A Tennants public house that closed and was left for a time unoccupied. The building has had some major alteration to the interior and exterior of the building but at the moment not sure whether it is going to be apartments or businesses.

THEN
c1980s

Fox House Hotel

11 Shirland Lane, S9

A Whitbreads Castle Eden house that closed in the late 1990s.

It was stated that Spence Broughton's wife looked out upon his gibbeted body from the upstairs window of this public house in the late 18th century.

A rather unlikely tale, especially geographically, plus we do not know if the pub or a predecessor was even built then.

There is a footnote to this story: A letter signed by Mrs Broughton was kept, framed, on one of the Fox House room walls for years. It was reported stolen in the mid 1960s. Could it possibly have been the genuine article?

NOW 2017

THEN c1980s

NOW
2017

Freedom View (aka Freedom, Freedom Hotel)

26 Walkley Road, S6

A wonderful looking building that has, since its closure as a public house, been developed into the King James Apartments. A further storey has been added onto the old Freedom View and I believe there are now eleven apartments in use.

A refurbishment that has been tastefully done.

THEN
c1980s

Freedom House

369-371 South Road, S6

The Freedom House was an old Whitbreads public house that has now been turned into two private dwellings.

The pub itself consisted of two pleasant rooms with a very comfortable lounge and a slightly smaller bar which housed a pool table.

THEN c2000s

NOW 2017

Friendship Inn

4 Tinsley Park Road - March Street, S9

A Stones Brewery public house that closed c2015 and left empty for a short time before being demolished, (right).

A good pub well frequented until the steel industry and slum clearance of the 1970s put the writing on the wall for this and many more Attercliffe pubs.

The Friendship stood across from the Fishermans Rest which was at 93 Tinsley Park Road.

Coleridge Road School was also situated on Tinsley Park Road.

THEN c1980s

Furnival

Verdon Street, S3

A fairly new build in public house terms, The Furnival was built in the 1960s and lasted only about 50 years before it was utilised for a more serious undertaking.

The Methodist Church in Sheffield is who now owns the old Furnival premises.

THEN
c1980s

NOW
2017

The Gate Inn

76-76 Attercliffe Common, S9

Attercliffe Common and Attercliffe Road had over 40 public houses situated on it from its start at Weedon Street until its end at the Wicker Arches.

The Gate was one of the more, shall we say, colourful pubs. Well known for some tough characters.

THEN
c1980s

Gate Inn

78 Penistone Road, S6

The Gate Inn was a feature of this part of Penistone Road along with the Travellers and Fletchers Bakery. In July 2006 the Bakery caught fire and and within a few years the two public houses were also closed and demolished.

Thankfully, Sainsbury's stepped in with a new supermarket build that seems to keeps the area thriving.

THEN
c1980s

George IV

216 Infirmary Road, S6

This old John Smiths pub is now being used as private dwellings. Opened 1828 - first closed 1992.

Desmond Peter Middleton born, January 1921, at the George IV was a founder member of the First SAS serving under Colonel Paddy Mayne. He later became a Maths and Science Teacher in Sheffield. Mentioned in the books The SAS in World War II by Gavin Mortimer and SAS with the Maquis June - September 1944 by Ian Wellsted. His sister Veda Gwendoline Middleton was reputed to be the first woman Head Teacher appointed in Sheffield when she became Head of Carbrook County Junior School. Veda Middleton was my fathers headteacher when he attended Carbrook County Junior School in the 1950s.

The Blitz Club, a music venue, was held above the George IV pub during in the 1970s.

Golden Ball

838 Attercliffe Road and Old Hall Road, Attercliffe, S9

The Golden Ball was renamed The Turnpike around the mid 1980s and sadly caught fire in 1989 and demolished soon after. In 1991 the Sheffield Stadium was built on part of the area that the Golden Ball once occupied. The stadium itself was later demolished to make way for new educational premises - still under construction when we are going to press

Gower Arms

47 Gower Street, Pitsmoor, S4

The Gower Arms was one of a good number of public houses in this area. The others being Staffordshire Arms, Grapes, Royal Oak all still serving. The Robin Hood, Albion, Carlisle Hotel, Crown, Norfolk Arms and East House have all closed their doors some time since. Now the Al-Saadi Supermarket which has tried, by the look of things, to cover the wonderful mosaic side panels either side of the door have taken ownership of the old pub.

Greyhound Inn

822 Attercliffe Road, S9

Built in 1884 when the steel industry was thriving. The Greyhound really tried to stay the distance to keep serving the Sheffield public but when most of the other pubs on this thoroughfare had given up the ghost it went the same way just leaving the Carlton as the only serving public house on Attercliffe Road.

As you can see Synergy-UK are now occupying the old Greyhound Inn.

THEN
c1980s

Hadfield Hotel

26/28 Barber Road, S10

A well frequented public house that seemed to have a secure future with all the student population in close proximity. But sadly it has gone the way of so many similar establishment and ended up as a Sainsbury's Local shop.

NOW
2017

Halfway House

80 Britannia Road, Darnall, S9

Public houses so named are generally on country roads and indicate stopping places for travellers. Probably at one time this would have been such a house. In some of the literature about the criminal Charles Peace it mentions that he may well have been a visitor to this establishment. Probably the previous building that stood here.

The old site is now left derelict, above.

THEN
c1980s

THEN
c1980s

NOW 2017

THEN c1990s

Hallamshire Hotel

155-157 Lydgate Lane, Crookes/Crosspool, S10

A Whitbreads public house that closed c2014 and was left for a time before being demolished and having accommodation, four houses built on the old site.

THEN c1980s

Hallcar

2 Carwood Terrace, S4

A Whitbreads public house that closed many years ago and is now being used as a private dwelling, (right).

Closed in 2009 and in 2010 there was some talk of the building being converted into apartments. Not sure if this happened.

The Hallcar was previously known as the Grove.

HALLCAR TAVERN

Hare and Hounds

27-29 Nursery Street, S3

A Stones public house that closed many years ago and left for a long time in a derelict state before being demolished. At the time of going to press the site is still derelict and boarded up.

The top image shows the old sign with just the letter H still visible amongst the rubble.

NOW
2017

THEN
c1990s

90

NOW 2017

THEN c1960s

Hare and Hounds

Church Street, Stannington, S6

The present, more modern, building that replaced the old Hare and Hound (shown middle) is now under threat of demolition itself. The pub has been closes a good few year and at the moment, mid 2017, there seems to be workmen delivering goods that will help turn it into the apartments we are led to believe are to be erected.

THEN c1990s

THEN c1980s

THEN c2000s

NOW 2017

Harlequin

26 Johnson Street, S3

A Wards public house that was previously know as the Harlequin and Clown. The pub used to be set just off the Wicker on Johnson Street. After or during demolition, top right, the license of the pub was transferred to the Manchester Hotel which is only a couple of hundred yards away on Nursery Street.

So technically, the Manchester Hotel disappeared and the Harlequin lives on.

THEN c1980s

Haychatter Inn

Bradfield Dale, Bradfield, S6

The Haychatter previously The Reservoir Inn was built soon after the Great Sheffield Flood in 1864 and served the men working on restoration of the dam.

The Haychatter closed its doors to the drinking public quite a few years ago and is now a private dwelling, the Haychatter House.

NOW 2017

THEN c1980s

NOW 2017

High Greave Inn

206 High Greave, Ecclesfield, S5

A Tetleys public house that closed and was soon taken over by John Heath & Sons a well known Sheffield Funeral Director.

The small image (centre) shows the High Greave having a new building finalised before the old pub is demolished.

THEN 1980s

Highway

Fox Street, Pitsmoor, S3

In historic terms the Highway is fairly modern in that it was built in 1963 and served the local drinkers for less that 40 years.

A nice cosy Stoned Brewery public house that closed, I believe, in the 1990s.

The site is now derelict, above.

THEN
c1980s

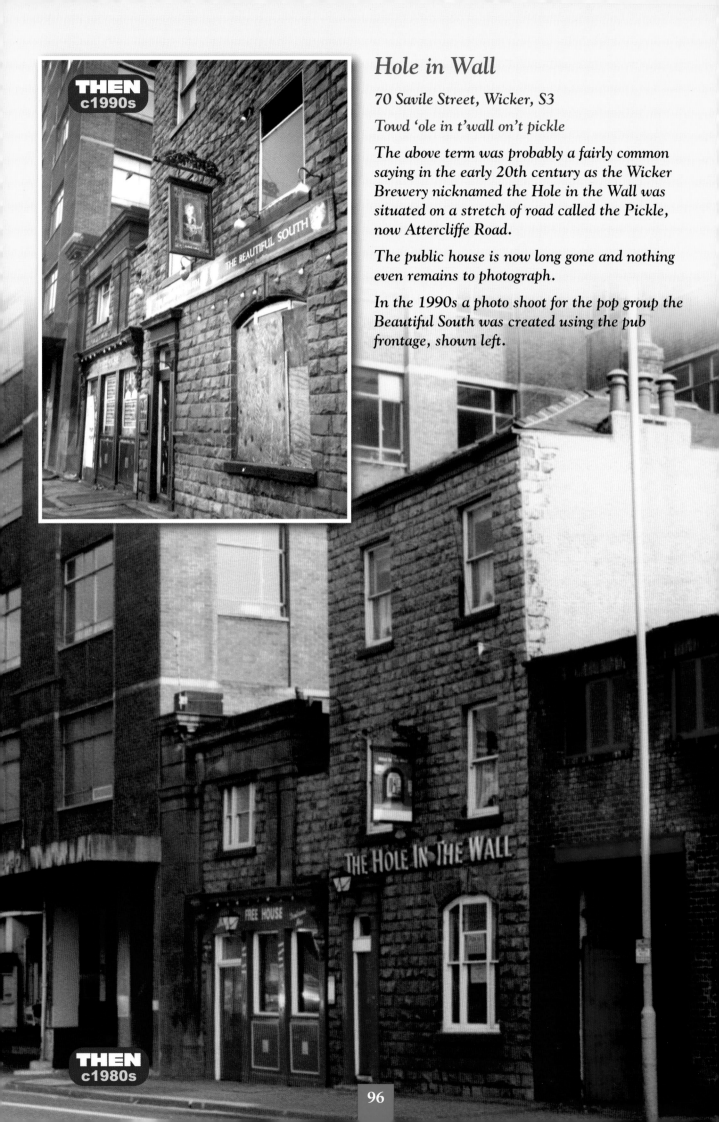

Hole in Wall

70 Savile Street, Wicker, S3

Towd 'ole in t'wall on't pickle

The above term was probably a fairly common saying in the early 20th century as the Wicker Brewery nicknamed the Hole in the Wall was situated on a stretch of road called the Pickle, now Attercliffe Road.

The public house is now long gone and nothing even remains to photograph.

In the 1990s a photo shoot for the pop group the Beautiful South was created using the pub frontage, shown left.

THEN
c1990s

THEN
c1980s

Hornblower *(aka Raven - O'Hagans)*

12-14 Fitzwilliam Street, S1

Originally called the Raven which at one time had a boxing gymnasium in the back of the pub. George Harvey Flood a well known local boxer and landlord ran it.

Later named The Hornblower and then finally before closure O'Hagans. The whole block was demolished to let the area see the redevelopments of the West One complex, top right.

Horse and Jockey

638 Attercliffe Road, S9

A John Smiths Magnet public house that closed many years ago and left for a time before being renovated by a local businessman who also redeveloped two other Attercliffe pubs, the Station and the Kings Head. After spending what must have been a vast amount of money the three pubs re-opened to a fanfare of activity and for a while the old Attercliffe dwellers came back in their droves. Sadly, this did not last and after a year or two the three pubs customer base diminished and all three have now closed their doors.

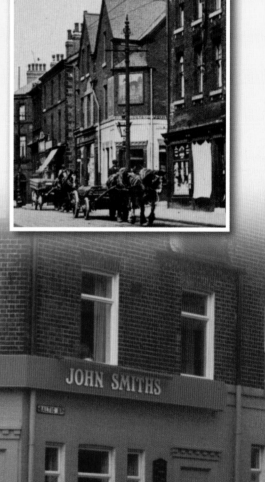

THEN c1920s

THEN c1980s

Horse and Lion

Norfolk Park Road, S2

The Horse and Lion was a William Stones public house that was a very fashionable public house in the 1960s-1970s. Along with the Fellbrigg and the Jervis Lum it became a regular Friday night out for my father and his friends.

Now all the three aforementioned pubs are no more, The Fellbrigg a place of religion, The Jervis Lum demolished and the Horse and Lion is now a Premier Supermarket, pictured above.

THEN
c1980s

Horseshoe Inn

279 Bellhouse Road, S5

The Horseshoe Inn was a William Stones Brewery public house and was one of about 10 drinking establishments in the Shiregreen, Firth Park area of Sheffield that have now all closed their doors.

The Sicey Hotel, Pheasant, Penguin, Shiregreen Hotel, Huntsman, Roman Ridge, Wharncliffe Hotel, Bellhouse WMC, Forum and Firth Park Hotel are now all closed as beer selling premises.

My parents, Ann and Mike had their engagement party on 12th October 1969 in the pub function room (hut) that is pictured above.

Huntsman

975 Barnsley Road, S5

A Tetleys public house that closed many years ago and was redeveloped to accommodate a block of flats, pictured left.

A nice two roomed establishment. The lounge was a lovely sizeable room which always seemed quiet and where you could sit in peace and enjoy your pint of Tetleys.

The tap room was a different story, noisy with some robust characters - entertaining none the less.

Industry Inn

89 Main Road, Darnall, S9

One of the many Wards public houses that were dotted throughout the Sheffield area.

A small pub that thrived all through the early part of last century.

Darnall pubs; The Meadow, Duke of York, Rose and Crown, Wellington and the Industry itself have all now closed their doors. I do believe all the buildings are still standing but now closed to the Sheffield drinking public.

NOW 2017

THEN c1980s

102

NOW
2017

Jervis Lum

Park Grange Drive, S2

A new build in the 1960s and served the Sheffield public for about 40 years before closure.

A Whitbread Brewery pub that was well frequented in the 1960s and 1970s.

At present 2017 the site is being redeveloped, above.

JERVIS LUM
WHITBREAD

THEN
c1970s

THE
JERVIS
LUM

THEN
c1980s

Jolly Buffer

144 Ecclesall Road, S11

Another of Sheffield shortlived public houses built c1980 and gone before its 25th birthday.

This Whitbreads public house had a relief carving in brick that was built into an exterior wall and entitled THE SHEFFIELD GRINDER AT HIS WHEEL, pictured right.

Sadly this important piece disappeared during redevelopment of the site.

The sculpture Walter Ritchie (born April 27th 1919; died on February 12th, 1997) is best known for his civic work. His most innovatory work was in brick.

It should be pointed out that the carving does not show a Buffer but a Grinder. It is strange that Ritchie didn't depict a Buffer Girl as this was the name of the public house.

Abdul's Indian Restaurant now occupies the old site, (top).

Junction Hotel

Station Road, Woodhouse, S13

A Tetleys public house that closed c2010s and was transformed into a NISA Local shop.

This large pub was situated next to Woodhouse train station and bus terminus. Open plan design, with large beer garden to rear and drinking area to front.

NOW 2017

THEN c1960s

Kings Head

709 Attercliffe Road, S9

Also know previously as the Champions Rest.

A John Smiths Magnet public house that was one of the last beer only houses in Sheffield.

The building was once home to an earthenware dealers, a chemist and obviously a pub.

Famous occupants are Samuel Jackson, of Spear and Jackson fame, George Littlewood who was a world champion endurance runner and landlord here at the beginning of the 20th century. Another landlord was Billy Calver a boxer of some repute who fought for a world championship in the 1960s.

The property now houses a pharmacy shown above.

THEN c1980s

THEN c1990s

Kings Head

Manchester Road, S10

A Whitbreads public house that closed after some controversy when locals tried their best to petition the sellers of the property to keep it as a public house. They lost their fight.

The land is now occupied by the flats/houses pictured right.

NOW 2017

THEN c1980s

Ladys Bridge Hotel

3 Bridge Street, S1

A Large public house that closed its doors to the Sheffield public in1993.

Previously know as Brewer on the Bridge and the Brewery Tap.

The pub was once the tap for the Whitbreads, Tennants brewery that was sited next to the public house.

Now The Adsetts Partnership business premises, left.

NOW 2017

THEN c1980s

NOW
2017

THEN
c1960s

Lambpool

291 Attercliffe Common, S9

The Lambpool was built c1870 and as you can gather from its name it gives evidence of the rural aspect of what Attercliffe was like in the late 19th century.

It survived until the later part of last century about 1989-1991.

The large island at Attercliffe Common and Janson Street now covers the spot where the Lambpool was sited.

THEN
c1980s

NOW 2017

Lansdowne Hotel

2 Lansdowne Road, S1

A public house that closed c1990s and redeveloped firstly as a petrol station and now as a large business complex, shown above.

The Hotel stood at the end of London Road at the junction with Lansdowne Road, opposite the Locarno/Lansdowne Cinema and was a very busy pub.

THEN c1970s

THEN c1980s

THEN
c1990s

Link

338 Hague Row, Park Hill, S2

The Link was built around 1961 when the Park Hill Flats were erected - the pub was built into the vast structure.

I believe the Link public house closed c2003.

TRADITIONAL CASK CONDITIONED ALES

THEN
2000s

THEN
c1980s

NOW 2017

Lion Hotel

2 Nursery Street, Wicker, S1

The Lion closed its doors as a public house in the mid 1980s and was turned into the Grosvenor Guest House. The Lion was a Tetleys pub and one of its last claims to fame (or infamy) was that in 1984 Arthur Hutchinson was convicted of a triple murderer of a well known Sheffield family.

Already on the run from prison he met a member of the family in the Lion and eventually returned home with them. After committing various other crimes he murdered three of the family. He went on the run for a few weeks before being caught. He received a life sentence and told that he would never be paroled. He is still in prison.

THEN c1980s